PEE-WEE'S GREY'S ANATOMY THE OFFICE THE SOPRANOS
PLAYHOUSE MAD MEN CHEERS
GET SMART GAME OF THRONES
ALL IN THE LOST THE HONEYMOONERS DEADWOOD
THE MARY TYLER MOORE SHOW BREAKING BAD
FAMILY CURB YOUR THE MAN THE TWILIGHT ZONE
ENTHUSIASM FROM U.N.C.L.E.

NAME That SHOW

100 Illustrated T.V. Show Puzzles

by PAUL ROGERS

CHRONICLE BOOKS
SAN FRANCISCO

Library of Congress Cataloging-in-Publication Data available

ISBN 978-1-4521-6113-6

Manufactured in China

Designed by Jill von Hartmann and Michael Morris

10 9 8 7 6 5 4 3 2 1

Chronicle Books LLC
680 Second Street
San Francisco CA 94107
www.chroniclebooks.com

Chronicle Books publishes distinctive books and gifts. From award-winning children's titles, bestselling cookbooks, and eclectic pop culture to acclaimed works of art and stationery, and journals, we craft publishing that's instantly recognizable for its spirit and creativity. Enjoy our publishing and become part of our community at www.chroniclebooks.com.

TO JILL

INTRODUCTION

Television is one of our great shared experiences. When I was growing up, in the years before all of today's viewing choices, my friends and I had to watch whatever was on whenever it aired. The next day we'd talk about the shows and try to remember details that seemed so important at the time. One pal would tape some of his favorite shows on a little audio cassette recorder, just to be able to listen later to the theme songs or save little bits of dialogue. I got a Polaroid camera and tried taking pictures of the screen to save certain images. Somewhere I've got a box of pictures of Jim Rockford's Firebird rolling down Wilshire Blvd. and Maxwell Smart's apartment. Paying close attention to the little moments like these got me started making drawings for my book *Name That Movie*, and now has led to this one, *Name That Show*.

Can you name a TV show from six scratchy drawings? In this collection, I've tried to generally avoid portraits of big stars, or drawings that are total giveaways in order to make these puzzles challenging, but not impossible to solve.

In *Name That Movie*, I was dealing with mostly two-hour time frames for each and looking for six things to draw that could spark the reader's memory of a film. But when a show stretches out over seasons, there are many more hours (and years) worth of individual moments that can make it harder for any one to stand out. Even so, I was surprised that I was able to conjure plenty of drawings that represent a single shot from a show that has remained in my memory for years. I've also included drawings of familiar objects that appeared in multiple episodes and have become icons of television culture. And I started to see little connections between shows decades apart. Who knew that VW buses have played such important roles in so many shows?

In choosing the six illustrations I'm hoping to conjure memories of the show rather than its narrative arc. Of course if you've never seen the show, it's unlikely you'll recognize it from these drawings. But as with *Name That Movie*, I hope the unfamiliar entries might pique your curiosity enough to seek them out, especially now that so many shows are so accessible worldwide. There are great shows here past and present, from the

1950s up to the new Golden Age of television. If you haven't seen *The Honeymooners*, or every episode of *The Wire*, you're in for a treat.

There are 100 shows in this book. The answers are given in two places in the back. There's a list of titles in the order that they appear in the book and there's also an alphabetical index. The alphabetical index is there for readers who don't want to inadvertently see the next title on the list when checking the answers. I hope you enjoy the book and find yourself paying a bit more attention to those small moments that make our favorite shows so memorable.

In the many long hours it took to do the research and make the 600 drawings in this book, at one point I was talking to another illustrator about the project. I might have been grumbling about the sheer amount of work involved. He reminded me that I shouldn't complain, "You've found the perfect job! You're getting paid to watch TV!"

—*Paul Rogers*

4

LIFE
SUPPORT
SYSTEMS

ALPHA
MOONBASE

WERNHAM
HOGG

9

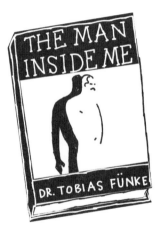

12

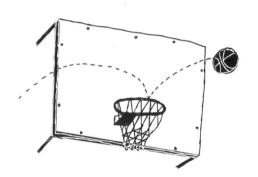

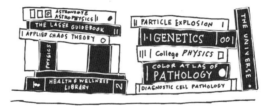

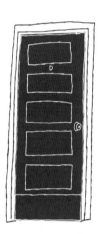

 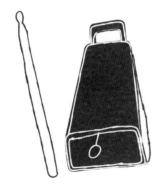 

25

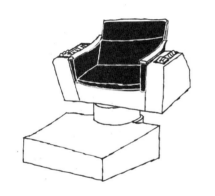

26

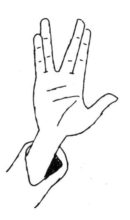

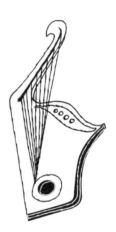

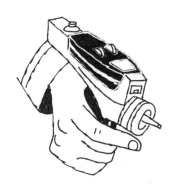  

27

  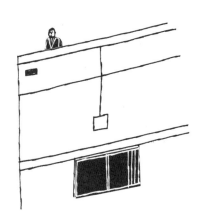

HOT WHIPPED CHOCOLATE

COFFEE

each cup INDIVIDUALLY brewed

noTIce!
TO ALL DRIVERS

DAY LINE

SHOW OR
PHONE BY
6 am

NIGHT LINE

SHOW OR
PHONE BY
3 pm

WELCOME BACK BOBBY

804

SUNSHINE CAB COMPANY

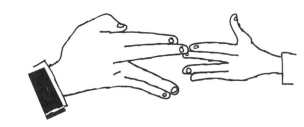

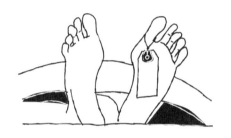  

BOSTON
SEOUL 34 mi / 54 km
CONEY ISLAND 7033 miles
SAN FRANCISCO 6428 miles
TOKYO 269 mi. / 414 km.
BURBANK 5610 miles
Death Valley 6776 miles
TOLEDO 8133
DECATUR 9412 m.

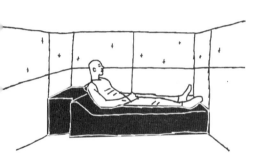  

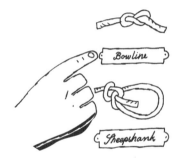

Tilly Weyl
Onlooker

Mixed Media: Human, wine glass, voice

POINT PLACE

VIKINGS
CLASS OF '77

41

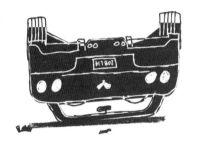 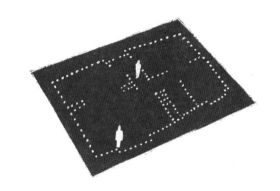 

44

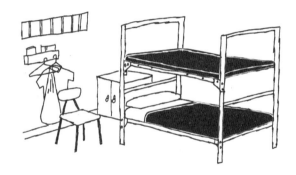  

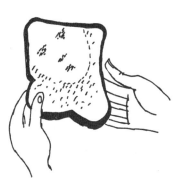

BORROWING OR
RECEIVING
COMMISSARY ITEMS
FROM ANYONE IS NOT
PERMITTED.

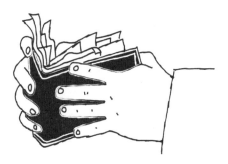

ssing	grilled peppers & onions 9.95	tomat
T	**RICHARD LEWIS**	CA
ey	whitefish, sable, capers, onions & cream cheese 8.95	turkey cheese
ese		
ER	**ROB REINER**	ME
	chopped liver, onions	liver

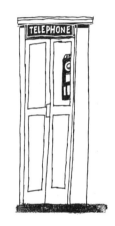

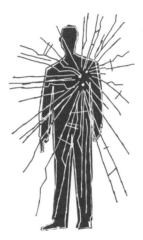

 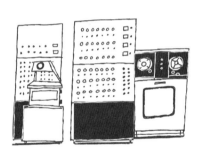 

52

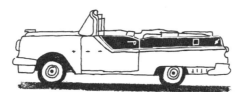 

BIGGEST BOX OFFICE SPLASH IN HISTORY!

$116,844,114

FIRST 3 DAYS AND STILL SWIMMING

VINCENT CHASE IS

JAMES CAMERON'S

AQUAMAN

Emergency exit

ZONA
RESTRIK

ENTRE
FERBATEN

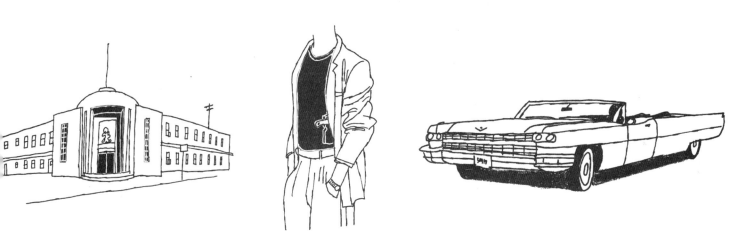

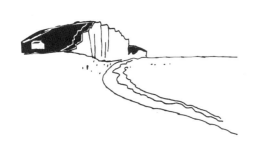

63

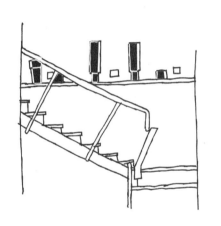

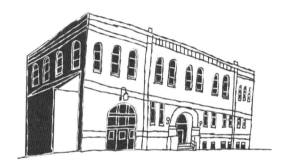

751

ROBERT HARTLEY Ph.D
PSYCHOLOGIST

GROUP
IN
SESSION

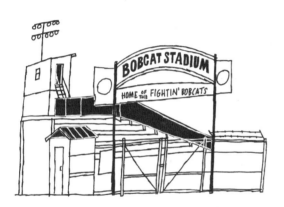

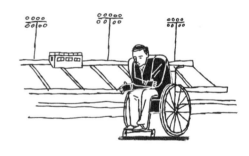

 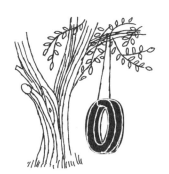 

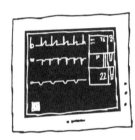 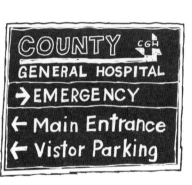 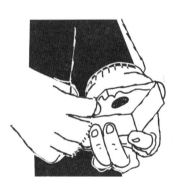

COUNTY CGH
GENERAL HOSPITAL
→ EMERGENCY
← Main Entrance
← Vistor Parking

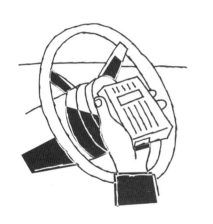  

74

ROOM ONE WEEK/NO GUESTS $3.00 week
$2.00
ROOM 2 FOLKS $1.50 day
DAY SLEEP $1.00 50¢
Half Day 60¢ 30¢
BATH/water Switch 50¢ 25¢

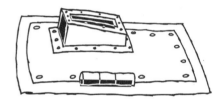

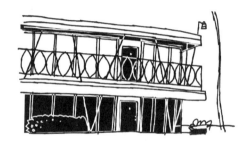

75

The Miami Tribune

LAURA MOSER

MOTHER OF TWO DIES

SLICE of LIFE

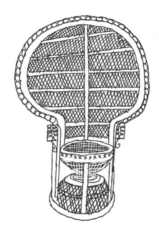

BEWARE
OF THE
THING

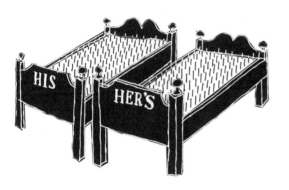  

80

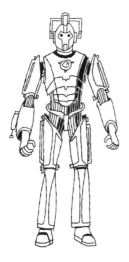

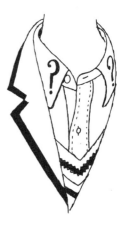

83

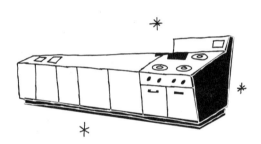

85

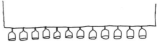

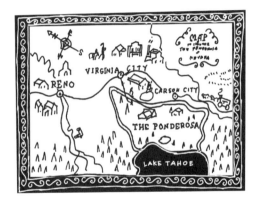

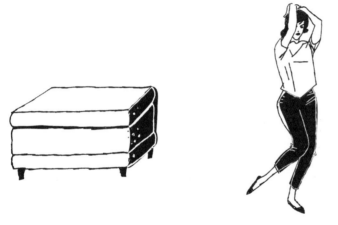
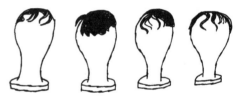

THE
PETE
STERNE
AMATEUR
HOUR

 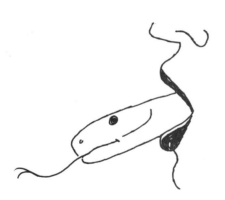 

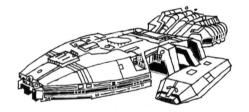

 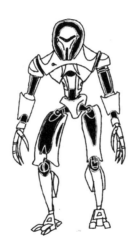 

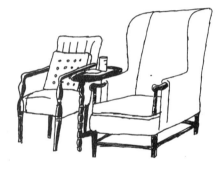

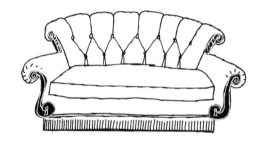

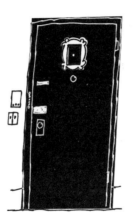

  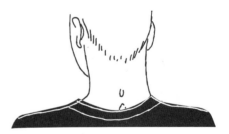

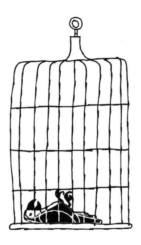

ANSWERS

1 Mad Men

 2 The Prisoner

 3 Stranger Things

 4 Downton Abbey

 5 I Dream of Jeannie

 6 Space: 1999

 7 The Office (UK)

 8 The Singing Detective

 9 The Walking Dead

 10 Arrested Development

 11 It's Always Sunny in Philadelphia

 12 The West Wing

13 Batman

 17 The Fresh Prince of Bel-Air

 21 The Big Bang Theory

 14 Daredevil

 18 The Wire

 22 The Wonder Years

 15 St. Elsewhere

 19 True Detective

 23 That Girl

 16 Empire

 20 Veep

 24 Saturday Night Live

25 House of Cards

 29 The Simpsons

 33 The Honeymooners

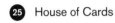 **26** Star Trek

 30 Taxi

 34 Six Feet Under

 27 The Avengers

 31 Mork & Mindy

 35 M*A*S*H

 28 The Office (US)

 32 Sex and the City

 36 Black Mirror

37 Portlandia

38 That 70s Show

39 Scandal

40 Modern Family

41 The Rockford Files

42 Northern Exposure

43 Grey's Anatomy

44 Orange Is The New Black

45 Seinfeld

46 Pee-Wee's Playhouse

47 I, Claudius

48 The Sopranos

49 Curb Your Enthusiasm

50 Get Smart

51 The Man from U.N.C.L.E.

52 Green Acres

53 Happy Days

54 I Love Lucy

55 Entourage

56 How I Met Your Mother

57 Mister Rogers' Neighborhood

58 The IT Crowd

59 Mission: Impossible

60 Miami Vice

61 Broadchurch

 65 The Twilight Zone

 69 MacGyver

 62 Homeland

 66 Absolutely Fabulous

 70 Friday Night Lights

 63 Sherlock

 67 Hill Street Blues

 71 Game of Thrones

 64 Leave It to Beaver

 68 The Bob Newhart Show

 72 ER

73 Freaks and Geeks

 77 Dexter

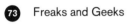 **81** Sons of Anarchy

 74 Deadwood

 78 Buffy the Vampire Slayer

 82 Dragnet

 75 The Golden Girls

 79 The Addams Family

 83 Gilligan's Island

 76 Lost

 80 Doctor Who

 84 Bewitched

85 Fawlty Towers

86 Cheers

87 Bonanza

88 The Dick Van Dyke Show

89 Breaking Bad

90 Twin Peaks

91 The Brady Bunch

92 American Horror Story

93 The Mary Tyler Moore Show

94 Battlestar Galactica

95 30 Rock

96 All in the Family

97 24

 98 Friends

 99 The X-Files

 100 Monty Python's Flying Circus

SHOW INDEX

PAUL ROGERS IS THE AUTHOR OF Name That Movie: 100 Illustrated Movie Puzzles. AN ILLUSTRATOR AND GRAPHIC DESIGNER, HIS WORK HAS BEEN FEATURED IN NUMEROUS PUBLICATIONS AND A VARIETY OF POPULAR CHILDREN'S BOOKS, AS WELL AS ON POSTAGE STAMPS AND ICONIC POSTERS. HE LIVES IN PASADENA, CALIFORNIA.

SIX FEET UNDER HOW I MET YOUR MOTHER DRAGNET
GREEN ROCKFORD FILES HAPPY DAYS
ACRES DAYS
I LOVE HOUSE OF CARDS I, CLAUDIUS LEAVE IT TO BEAVER
MIAMI VICE
LUCY GOLDEN GILLIGAN'S ISLAND FAWLTY
GIRLS TOWERS
THE WIRE
THE WONDER YEARS SEINFELD SHERLOCK
TRUE DETECTIVE TWIN X-FILES
PEAKS